Kim Campbell

The keener who broke down barriers

Written by Heather Grace Stewart
Illustrated by Thomas Dannenberg

Credits.
JackFruit would like to thank Merna Forster for the photograph that appears on the title page, Mike Lukovich and the Creators Syndicate for the political cartoon on page 17. Thank you to Dan Morris for the cartoon beavers that appear throughout this book.

JackFruit Press Ltd.
Toronto, Canada
www.jackfruitpress.com

Library and Archives Canada Cataloguing in Publication

Grace Stewart, Heather, 1972–
    Kim Campbell: the keener who broke down barriers / Heather Grace Stewart; Thomas Dannenberg, illustrator.

(Canadian prime ministers: warts & all)
Includes index.
ISBN 978-0-9736407-0-0

1. Campbell, Kim, 1947–   —Juvenile literature. 2. Canada—Politics and government—1993–2003—Juvenile literature.
3. Prime ministers—Canada—Biography—Juvenile literature.
I. Dannenberg, Thomas, 1957– II. Title. III. Series.

FC631.C34G73 2007   j971.064'7092   C2007-904589-8

Printed and bound in Canada

...So, I'm here to show you around this really cool series of books on great Canadians.

This book tells the story of Kim Campbell, Canada's 19th prime minister.

She overcame prejudices, personal problems, and political setbacks to become Canada's first female prime minister.

Contents

Hot topics

Kim Campbell: In the right

What kind of person is Canada's first woman prime minister? Whether they like her or not, many people describe her as having a colourful personality. Her determination to stay true to her beliefs, even when those beliefs are controversial, shows that she is a gutsy lady!

TD07

place at the wrong time

Articulate. Aloof. Abrasive. Ambitious. Arrogant. Each of these adjectives has been used at one time or another to describe Kim Campbell, Canada's first female prime minister.

So, what kind of person is she, really? It depends on whom you ask. Reporters have described her as "brash and calculating". Some say she had the charismatic presence of former British prime minister **Margaret Thatcher** (who was also known as the "Iron Lady") combined with the flamboyance of Canada's former red-rose-sporting prime minister **Pierre Elliott Trudeau**. One writer described her as "dedicated, witty, vibrant, and clever" yet "dismissive of those who do not share her view of the world." Former Canadian prime minister Brian Mulroney says she is "very vain." Others have said that she is simply shy.

One thing is certain, however. Kim Campbell was first to create a recipe for becoming a Canadian female prime minister, and so far, she remains the only one to do so.

What was Kim Campbell's recipe for becoming prime minister? Start with a girl who isn't afraid to be different from other girls her age, who is 12 when her mother leaves the family,

Want to know more? The words in bold are explained in the glossary at the back of the book.

Kim considers herself a forward-thinking person with a good sense of humour. She has joked that if she didn't have a knack for noticing the funny things in life, she might have gone crazy during her time in politics, mainly due to the pressure of being Canada's first female PM.

Kim always seemed to do her best, from the 10-year-old television reporter to her present positions speaking all over the world.

and who is therefore forced to grow up quickly. Add in a job in British Columbia cleaning smelly fish, a failed year at university yet spectacular results at law school later in life. Then gently stir in self-discipline, the ability to play cello and to speak some Russian, French, and German, and a preference for classical music (along with a willingness to give country line-dancing a try).

Combine them with a belief that women need to be in government because they experience the world differently from men. Finally, mix in the self-assuredness required to speak your mind when the whole nation is listening with the ability to poke fun at oneself and to find the humour in bad situations.

Do all that and whom do you get? Kim Campbell, Canadian prime minister from June 25 to November 3, 1993.

Making choices

Kim Campbell has left her mark in the history books as North America's first female leader of a nation, and, at 46, one of the youngest women to assume office in any country.

As justice minister, she guided twenty-six bills through **Parliament**. The way Kim went about drafting the guidelines for some laws reflected her self-described style of politics, "the politics of inclusion." When making decisions, she did what no one had done before—she consulted with, and included the opinions of, regular citizens, as well as ministry officials.

As prime minister, Kim reorganized Parliament for the 1990s. Hers was the most radical restructuring of cabinet since Confederation. She created several important new departments, including **human resources**. This reflected her commitment to her campaign promise to improve the organization of government departments and their policies.

But she spent more energy in her few months in 1993 as prime minister trying to fix misunderstandings created by her difficult relationship with the media than realizing her dream of transforming democracy in Canada.

"I will always be haunted by questions of what I could have done differently that fateful summer of 1993," she wrote in her autobiography.

If Kim had made other choices that summer as PM or led a different leadership campaign that fall, would she have stayed on longer as prime minister of Canada? Read on and decide for yourself.

As North America's first female leader of a nation, Kim Campbell has left her mark in the history books. At 46, she is one of the youngest women to assume office in any country. But that certainly isn't all she should be remembered for.

Kim spent a lot of time trying to fix misunderstandings created by her difficult relationship with the media. They commented on her hair, her outfits, and her personality in ways that many think were based on her gender rather than her ability to run the country. But Kim created a lot of the problems herself. She had the habit of speaking first, without considering how her words would be interpreted by the many Canadians listening.

Originally named Avril Phaedra, Kim is often teased because of her unusual first names. But her mother reassures her that being different from other people is good and not something to be afraid of.

Avril also stands out because of her above-average vocabulary and her confidence. At age 10, she becomes one of the hosts of CBC's *Junior Television Club*.

Chapter 1

Not like the others

1947
Avril Phaedra Douglas (Kim) Campbell is born on March 10 in Port Alberni, BC.

1959
Avril's mother leaves her family.

Avril changes her name to Kim.

1964
Kim enrolls at the University of British Columbia.

1969
Kim graduates with a Bachelor of Arts (BA) in political science.

1970
Kim begins a doctorate program at the London School of Economics (LSE).

Avril Phaedra Douglas Campbell was born in the town of Port Alberni, British Columbia, on March 10, 1947. Her mother, Phyllis Cook (nicknamed Lissa), was the daughter of Scottish immigrants who had settled near Nanaimo Lake in 1911. Lissa chose the name Avril (French for April) for her daughter's first name because that was the month her daughter was due to be born. Douglas was the name of Lissa's youngest brother. Lissa chose Phaedra, which refers to an unlucky queen in ancient Greek mythology, because she liked the way it sounded.

At an early age, Avril felt different from other kids. They teased her because she had an unusual name, an above-average vocabulary, and used lots of words they didn't. But she wasn't alone: her older sister, Alix, was in the same boat. Lissa assured her daughters, however, that it was good to be honest and to be yourself and if you could do that, then the opinons of others should not matter.

By the time Avril was 10 years old and in grade five, her differences landed her a spot on television. In 1957 she became one of the regulars on the CBC children's show *Junior Television Club*. She interviewed guests and learned a lot about how television programmes are made.

"Mom's gone" . . . and so is Avril

A crushing blow came to Avril just two years later. She was 12 years old and away with her sister, Alix at **boarding school**—St. Anne's Academy—in Victoria, British Columbia. After receiving a letter from their father, her sister called Avril to her room. "Mom's gone," she told Avril gently. Avril thought "gone" meant "dead." But, no, Alix explained: their mother had left their father.

It would be 10 years before Avril saw her mother again. Lissa sent letters to her daughters, but the **nuns** at their Catholic boarding school withheld them, judging that it was best for the girls. Their father didn't visit the girls to console them or speak with them about this huge loss in their lives. Hurt and confused, Avril changed her name to Kim. She knew it was a name her mother had liked but had put aside when a friend had chosen it for her newborn son.

The loss of her mother changed Kim to the core. It made her heart feel, as she says, "squeezed and wrung dry for a time." During her high school years at Prince of Wales Secondary School, in Vancouver, Kim seemed happy and well-adjusted, but inside, she felt like a freak.

Her father and Alix could not hide how they felt and Kim was desperate that her remaining family not fall apart. She became extremely self-reliant and an over-achiever. As she didn't have a mother whose approval she could strive for and her father wouldn't communicate with her, she tried to win recognition in high school. She was extremely successful, graduating in 1964 as valedictorian, winning the English prize and the Girl's Merit Award for best all round girl student, and becoming the school's first female student council president.

Handling a "man's job" just fine

In the fall of 1964 Kim became a student of the University of British Columbia (UBC) and had her first venture into politics. She ran for election as the president of UBC's Frosh Council. A woman running a campaign against two men was practically unheard of in those conservative times. Kim handled sexist comments on campus and in the student newspaper (such as "a girl can't handle a man's job") like a pro. "Rise, women, let's tidy up the world," she wrote in response.

As Kim's first year progressed, students on campus were rallying against the **Vietnam War** and fighting for equality for women. Kim got involved as she whole heartedly agreed with the anti-war movement. She also started to devour **feminist** literature, like **Betty Friedan**'s *The Feminine Mystique* and **Simone de Beauvior**'s *The Second Sex*.

Life after her mother left was very confusing for young Avril. She was only 12 years old—can you imagine just how devastated she must have been?

She decided to change her name to Kim and, because her father and sister were falling apart, she felt she had to be the strong one—the one that would hold their sad family together. She became a top student, excelling at everything she put her mind to.

She once said: "I felt that I had to be good at things or people wouldn't like me"

Twelve-year-old Avril changes her name to Kim right after her mother sends a note to her and her sister at their boarding school, explaining that she can no longer stay with their father. It will be 10 years before Kim will see her again.

1959

11

Kim, the wonder girl of the 50-cent words, FAILED A YEAR AT UNIVERSITY!

Unimaginable, eh?

Kim actually thinks failing that year was the best thing that could have happened to her. It helped her get a handle on her emotional turmoil and focus on what she really wanted to do with her life.

She won't have halibut

Getting through university was tough academically and emotionally for Kim—but also financially. Although her father earned a good living as a crown prosecutor, she was expected to pay for her own studies. To earn some money for her tuition, Kim worked at a fish-packing plant in Prince Rupert during the summer after her first year of university, earning $1.82 per hour. Her job was to put pieces of halibut into small boxes and scrub the freezer clean with a long-handled brush.

This tough job opened her eyes to the double standard of the workplace. Many of the hardworking women at the plant were paid less than the men and rarely got promoted to the better jobs. As a result of that job, Kim will not eat halibut!

Mrs. Vroom, I presume?

The first two years of university were among the most troubled of Kim's life. She had poor study habits and found it difficult to work at home, where her father and his second wife, Ginny, were often arguing. Instead, she spent the start of her university career whooping it up with her friends. As a result, the girl who had been high school valedictorian ended up failing her second year of university. Yikes! She moved in with a close friend of her sister's and went on to repeat the year successfully.

After a total of five years at university, Kim finished her degree in 1969. Her mother had missed watching Kim grow into a young woman, but now she made an effort to attend her daughter's graduation. She flew in with her second husband, Bill Vroom, from their home in the **West Indies** to attend the ceremony. On that special summer day, Kim saw her mother again for the first time in a decade.

Heading overseas—alone

Kim developed a keen interest in politics and applied to study **international relations** at the prestigious London School of Economics (LSE) in London, England. She was offered a **fellowship**, but had a difficult choice to make.

You see, Kim had started a romantic relationship with a UBC math professor, **Nathan Divinsky**. His family and friends called him Tuzie. Although he was 22 years older than Kim, they became very close and shared a love of music.

Tuzie wanted her to stay and marry him, but Kim knew she would gain so much by accepting the position at LSE. She also believed that the love she and Tuzie shared could survive the ocean between them for a couple of years. As self-reliant as ever, Kim headed off to London that autumn on her own.

After five years at university, Kim finishes her four-year honours BA. Her mother, who'd missed watching Kim grow into a young woman, makes an effort to attend her daughter's graduation. She flies in with her second husband, Bill, from their home in the West Indies.

On that special summer day, Kim sees her mother again for the first time in a decade. She feels awkward about meeting her stepfather while her father is present, but despite some "mixed emotions," the day goes well. When Lissa and Bill move back to Vancouver Island in 1970, Kim and her mother begin rebuilding their relationship. Over the years it will grow into one that was "gratifying" for both of them.

1971

While studying at England's London School of Economics, she begins to get a sense of her own politics. She believes that women should have a bigger role in deciding how the world should be run. Kim takes part in a women's liberation march to Trafalgar Square.

Chapter 2

An MP in the making

Kim did a lot of growing up in her years abroad. While studying at the London School of Economics (LSE), she began to get a sense of her own ideas of how things should be run, how governments should operate, and the rights and responsibilities of citizens. It became crystal clear that she was a feminist; Kim felt that women should have a bigger presence in governments and in deciding how the world should be run. Feminism was a new thing and women all over the world were taking to the streets to demonstrate their belief that women should receive the same opportunities and wages as men. In 1971, Kim participated in her first demonstration, a **women's liberation** march from London's Hyde Park Corner to Trafalgar Square.

Kim took an exciting three-month study trip to the Communist-run **Union of Soviet Socialist Republics (USSR)** in April of 1972. This opened her eyes to other political systems and also gave her a chance to practise the Russian she had learned at University of British Columbia (UBC).

When her studies in the USSR ended, Kim continued working on the research required for her doctoral (graduate) degree, but she also moved onto a new project: planning her wedding to Tuzie. The two were married on September 15, 1972 at the Hampstead Registry Office in London. They lived for a year in London where they were joined by Tuzie's teenaged daughters Mimi and Pamela.

1972
Kim marries Nathan Divinsky.

1973
Kim leaves the London School of Economics before finishing her thesis.

1975
Kim begins lecturing at the University of British Columbia.

1979
Kim begins lecturing at Vancouver Community College.

1980
Kim studies law at UBC.

She is elected as a trustee of the Vancouver school board.

1983
Kim is called to the bar of British Columbia.

She divorces Nathan.

She becomes chair of the Vancouver school board.

1984
Kim runs as a Social Credit party candidate, but loses.

She becomes vice-chair of the Vancouver school board.

1985
Kim becomes director of BC premier William Bennett's office.

15

What did Kim do as a trustee that got her noticed? Kim got noticed because she was very good at finding ways to slash the budget even when parents cried out for more funding.

She is also known to have taken money away from programs for kids with special needs and giving it to "future leaders" — the kids in "gifted" programs. While no one doubts that gifted kids need money too, can you imagine the amount of flack she would get for making such a controversial move today?

An instant family and a first real home

Kim enjoyed getting to know her stepdaughters better, especially Pamela, who was about the same age that Kim had been when her mother had left. Kim did all she could to make a nice home for the girls that year. She realized later that the bonding that went on that year was emotionally good for her as well as the girls. Plus, she discovered that she enjoyed cooking.

The couple returned to Vancouver a year later, in August 1973, so Tuzie could begin teaching mathematics at UBC that fall. Kim started teaching at UBC in 1975 and then later at Vancouver Community College. Kim and Tuzie had lots of friends and were often entertaining people in their new home. Unsurprisingly, teaching and these other activities became the focus of Kim's life and she never finished the research she needed to complete her graduate degree.

In the summer of 1980 she was asked by the **Vancouver Non-Partisan Association** (NPA) to run as a candidate for the school board. Kim agreed. After studying politics for so many years, she wanted to find out if she had what it took to actually become a politician. She was elected as a **trustee** of the Vancouver School Board. It would end up being a smart move: school board politics gave her a chance to practice speaking in public and to learn many of the skills required to be a politician.

Big changes

They were exciting years career wise, but the late seventies brought many emotional crises for Kim. Her stepfather Bill had open-heart surgery and died 24 hours later. Soon after, David, the husband of her sister Alix, died unexpectedly at the young age of 32. In addition, Kim and Tuzie were unable to have children. These tragedies created much sadness in the household. Kim and Tuzie were growing apart. The couple separated in 1982 and divorced in 1983.

But Kim didn't let these personal troubles stop her. She decided a law degree could help her if she ever wanted to make a move into provincial or even national politics. So in 1980, at age 32, Kim started law school at UBC while still working as a trustee at the Vancouver School Board.

A new verdict

As a trustee of the board, and eventually chairperson in 1982, Kim was concerned about the board's overspending taxpayers' dollars, and she was dead set against an illegal Vancouver teachers' strike.

But she had not yet learned that the key rule of politics is never to offend people. As a result, many of her opponents found her "haughty," "rude," and "arrogant." Some even called her a bully. But other colleagues felt she

Media Matters:
The Press vs. Politicians

Politicians have long complained that the press skews what they say and do by using certain words and images and omitting others. On the other hand, members of the press often argue that politicians manipulate them, so the public will view them in a more favourable light.

In the 1990s, Kim Campbell became the first female PM to face a press she felt misrepresented her comments. She felt they were more critical of her because she was a woman. For example, the media would make negative comments about her hair or her suits, but reporters rarely mentioned the hair or suits of male politicians. Kim definitely wasn't the first politician who felt the press were at times biased, and she certainly isn't the last.

Prime Minister Pierre Elliott Trudeau had very public disagreements with the Parliamentary Press Gallery (reporters who specialize in covering parliament) during most of his time as PM. He felt the stories they reported were biased, so in turn he tried to control their reporting by only speaking with journalists and media organizations that he preferred and trying to avoid giving interviews to those reporters that he felt might misrepresent or twist his words.

Like most politicians and the press, Trudeau and the media had a symbiotic relationship: while they likely didn't like each other very much, the journalists

Mike Lukovich/Creators Syndicate

needed him to sell papers, and he needed them to get his messages to the Canadian people.

More recently, Prime Minister **Stephen Harper** and the Parliamentary Press Gallery had a big public conflict. In May 2006, his staff tried to manage news conferences by selecting which reporters could ask questions. As a result, the press gallery staged a boycott, and about two dozen members walked out on a Harper event when he wouldn't take their questions. As a result, the walkout became the news story, and Canadians did not get to hear what Harper wanted them to hear. Instead the newspapers, television reports, and radio stories suggested that Harper was preventing reporters from getting information that they felt Canadians should know.

Later, the Conservative PM alleged that some Press Gallery members held an anti-Conservative bias. "I have trouble believing that a Liberal prime minister would have this problem," he said, "But the press gallery at the leadership level has taken an anti-Conservative view." He then announced that he would no longer give news conferences for the national media or the Press Gallery, and would now only speak to local media.

When you closely examine how the press and politicians dance around each other, it seems a lot like a marionette show. Who do you think is truly pulling the strings these days?

For more information about politics and the press, visit our website at www.jackfruitpress.com.

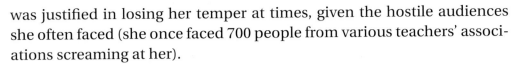

was justified in losing her temper at times, given the hostile audiences she often faced (she once faced 700 people from various teachers' associations screaming at her).

In February 1983, during her last year of law school, Kim was approached by someone from the **Social Credit (Socred) party**, the party that governed the province of British Columbia. The premier had noticed Kim's work as a trustee and liked the cost-cutting measures Kim had taken with the school board. Kim was asked to run as a Socred candidate for Vancouver Centre in the upcoming provincial election.

Should she go for it? Kim wanted to run in the provincial election, but it would overlap with the writing of her final law exams. Kim accepted the challenge. She wasn't sure which made her more nervous: writing six difficult law-school exams during the campaign or asking strangers on the street for their vote!

The campaign was difficult, especially in Vancouver's downtown east side where the **New Democratic Party** (NDP) had always ruled the roost. People actually threw things at Kim and her campaign workers! But Kim remained strong and worked hard during her campaign—although at times she was still quick to lose her temper.

Some you win, some you lose

Still, it wasn't a surprise to Kim when she passed her law exams but lost the election. Although the Socred party won a strong majority in the province, Kim and her co-candidate were trounced by the NDP candidates in her riding. Kim chalked it up to a good learning experience, and she continued on with her plans for a life in law. After stepping down as school board chairperson to a less time-consuming role as vice-chairperson of the school board, she thought she would end her political career to focus on law.

But during a trip to see friends in Ottawa in 1985, a law school classmate who worked on Parliament Hill called it differently. She gave Kim a full tour of the Hill and said she could see her working there one day as a **member of Parliament (MP)**. "This is where you belong," she told Kim.

Her friend was right. It would simply take Kim a few years to arrive.

Kim sure did have a lot of "balls in the air". She was divorcing Tuzie while trying to forge a relationship with her stepdaughters. Plus she was studying for her very difficult law exams while trying to win her first election.

Angry voters throw things at Kim and her campaign workers as they canvas for votes in downtown Vancouver.

1983

When Premier Bill Bennett steps down, Kim decides to campaign for his job. Her career-long troubles with the media begin with a mean-spirited article in the Vancouver Sun.

"Maybe you need a hearing aid" Campbell tells reporters

Are words of two syllables difficult for you to understand? I hope those scabs on your knuckles aren't distressing you too much

Taking her comments out of context, the article has Kim describing herself as a "gifted person" who prefers the company of her intellectual equals but claims to like ordinary people, the kind "who sit in their undershirt and watch the game on Saturday, beer in hand." The article also quotes her as saying "I suppose (these people) would find me as boring as I would find them."

"I do have an IQ in three digits, and I'm prepared to stand up in House...

Campbell says she finds average voter boring.

Chapter 3

Why not?

1986
Kim runs for leader of the BC Social Credit party, but loses.

She wins a seat in the provincial legislature.

Kim marries Howard Eddy.

1988
Kim runs and wins a seat in the House of Commons as a member of the Progressive Conservative party.

It was just another annual meeting of the Canadian Bar Association (CBA), but that gathering in the summer of 1985 got the ball rolling in two major areas of Kim's life.

First, it was where she met Howard Eddy, a 45-year-old lawyer from Victoria, BC. The pair quickly formed a serious relationship; by the next spring they were talking about marriage. Second, at that same meeting she was offered a job as executive director of the office of **Bill Bennett**, BC premier and Socred party leader.

Kim was excited as her new job would allow her to use some of her growing legal knowledge, plus perhaps help her figure out if and how she could return to politics in the future. She eagerly joined Bennett's office at that summer's end.

The very next May, Bennett announced he was stepping down as leader of the BC Socreds. During Kim's nine months working in the premier's office, she had learned a great deal about running a government. Now she wanted to be more than an executive director for the premier: she wanted to run for his position!

Ready to run

Kim wondered if she had enough experience to run for leadership of the Socred party, especially as she would be up against **Bill Vander Zalm**. Nicknamed "The Zalm," this charismatic politician had been a minister in Bennett's cabinet for eight years. But Bud Smith, principal

Brave or what? Kim stood up to her boss—The Zalm—and practically called him a liar when he tried to change the rules to help one of his friends get rich! Kind of reduces one's chances of getting promoted, don't you think?!

But Kim wasn't going to hide her views, just to get on The Zalm's good side. She told a Vancouver *Sun* columnist, "I'm not prepared to sell my soul to get into Cabinet."

secretary to Premier Bennett, was also running for the leadership without ever having run for any political position before. If he could do it, Kim thought, why couldn't she?

Kim plunged into the campaign race, learning the ropes as she went along and gratefully receiving financial support from friends. She didn't really think she could win, but she wanted to make a name for herself in BC politics.

Kim bashing

The media got on Kim's case, publishing a negative article about her that presented her comments in a way that made her look bad. But nevertheless, on speech night at the leadership convention that July, Kim spoke well, and the public could see what she was really like (as compared to the horrible newspaper articles), plus they liked the vision she had for the future of the Socred party. While she didn't win the leadership convention —Bill Vander Zalm became premier—Kim's speech received the only standing ovation of the night.

The year 1986 brought two more life-changing events for Kim: she married Howard in August, and in October she ran another campaign. This time she was trying to win a seat as a Socred candidate in the provincial legislature. The campaign was a tough fight, but on election night, she was introduced by a fellow Socred as "a new political star in B.C." She had won!

Kim was now a rookie **member of the Legislative Assembly** (MLA). Though new, she was quick to take on the many duties her job entailed. In her two years as an MLA she brought about several changes that positively affected minorities in her community. "For example, she worked with the health minister to make provisions for people with AIDS (Aquired Immune Deficiency Syndrome) and to reduce ignorance about the disease. She also helped the Kamloops Indian band protect their physical heritage through Project Pride, the task force on heritage conservation that she chaired.

A style of her own

It was during this time as an MLA that Kim developed her own political style. She proved time and again that she was feisty and unafraid to speak out on controversial issues. She was also extremely ambitious and tried to get ahead, even though it sometimes made her appear aggressive. But she didn't care how she appeared; she was there to make a difference.

These qualities would soon help Kim make national headlines—much to her own surprise—as she butted heads with Premier Bill Vander Zalm, the leader of her own party! Kim often disagreed with the premier's views and

Controversy, Controversy!

Controversy happens when different people openly disagree about a matter of opinion. Controversies vary in size from private disputes between just two people, to large-scale disagreements between cultures and societies.

Religion and politics are the main reasons why controversies take place in our society, and because Canadians are different in so many ways, there are several other reasons controversies first emerge, like philosophy and ethnicity. The media almost always has a role to play in a controversy. They are often the first to expose a private controversy to others, making the "buzz" (the way the news spreads) and the scale of a minor controversy even greater.

For example, people have fought wars over freedom of speech; privacy and safety on the internet are subjects that often spark debate. In Toronto, Ontario these two issues collided when four students were arrested in a protest over postings on the highly popular website, Facebook.com.

Facebook.com, a popular social networking website, originally began as a site for college students to interact. In Feburary 2006 it was opened so that anyone can now participate and by June 2007, it was ranked amongst the top 20 sites visited on the entire Internet! So how would you feel if someone criticized you in such a public way? Well, the vice-principal of a Toronto school suspended five different students for posting criticisms about him. Later that week, approximately a dozen friends of the students decided to protest their suspension in front of the school. The protest soon ballooned to over 100 students protesting their right to free speech and four students were arrested.

The vice-principal felt his privacy and safety were violated by the postings while the students felt they had a right to their opinions and stood their ground, even when to do so meant they risked going to prison.

Kim always stood her ground when faced with a controversy. She never backed down on an issue she felt strongly about just to win votes.

She showed strength of character when facing her political opponents, and even within her own political party! She publically disagreed with her boss in Vancouver and although she knew it could limit her ability to get ahead under his leadership, she still stood her ground. She even said to a reporter, "I'm not prepared to sell my soul to get into Cabinet".

As you can imagine, this did not endear her to her boss! Kim decided to enter federal politics instead. But Kim's battles with controversy did not end in Vancouver—wherever she went, Kim would speak her mind, often to the advantage of people who did not have a voice themselves. As justice minister she was not afraid to speak out for **First Nations peoples'** rights, those of people in same-sex relations and women's issues. Kim managed *to get things changed to improve things where other politicians would have been afraid to speak out.*

For more information about this topic, visit our website at www.jackfruitpress.com.

Here's another one of the double standards: When men fight back they are seen as assertive, but when women do the same they are seen as pushy or aggressive.

actions. She believed that he frequently changed his opinion to suit whomever he was speaking to, and she disapproved. Sometimes she even found herself speaking out against him. For example, in 1987, Vander Zalm tried to alter the bidding process for the sale of Vancouver's **Expo '86** lands to permit his friend to bid after the official closing date. This was against the rules. When this was revealed, Kim spoke up in the Conservative caucus, challenging Vander Zalm's explanation of his actions.

In addition, Kim openly supported public funding for abortions (a way to end a pregnancy) and freedom of choice for women. The Zalm, on the other hand, was against this and in 1988 decided not to provide funding for abortions in BC. Kim was the only one of her colleagues to speak out publicly against the premier's decision.

Goodbye kisses

When people said she could kiss her chances goodbye of getting into Cabinet, thanks to this very public stand, she said she didn't care. Kim told reporters that she was sad to see her expression of her honest views taken as such a "remarkable thing."

Soon Kim realized she'd never feel at home in Vander Zalm's government. She did not agree with his politics, she felt he was dishonest, and she did not feel comfortable with him as leader of the party. It was time for a change—a party change.

Her opportunity came when a key player in BC's **Progressive Conservative** (PC) party asked her to consider being the party's candidate in Vancouver Centre in the next federal election. **Brian Mulroney**'s PC government was seeking re-election. After months of reflection, Kim decided that perhaps she could do more for B.C. at the federal level of politics, on **Parliament Hill** in Ottawa, than "beating my head against a brick wall in Victoria" under Vander Zalm's leadership.

Kim campaigned hard, and at 4 a.m. on November 22, 1988, the day after the federal election, a Vancouver *Sun* reporter called and woke her up with positive news. The vote counting had just been completed—she'd won the seat by 269 votes.

Kim was off to Ottawa!

Kim finds herself in the media's spotlight once again. But now she is television news. Anti-free-trade demonstrators are shouting her down. She points her finger at them and shouts right back.

"Why are you so scared?"

Kim is embarrassed when she sees her outburst on television! She finds her voice "shrill" but to her surprise, her supporters say they love how she looks and sounds. Some later say that this image—played again and again on television—won her the election.

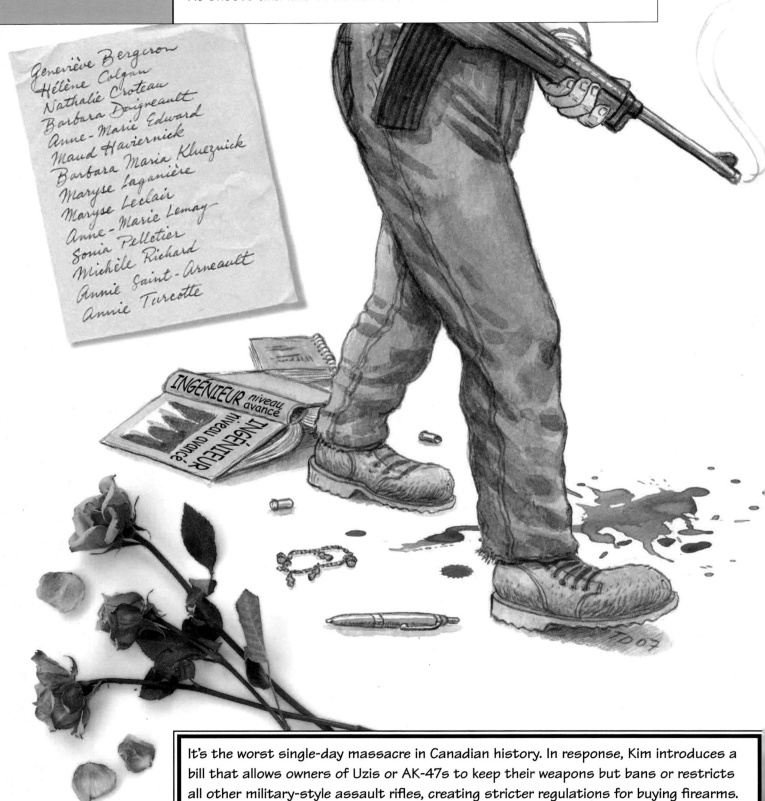

1989

On December 6, an armed and enraged man enters Montreal's École Polytechnique screaming, "Je hais les feministes." ("I hate feminists.") He shoots and kills 14 women and then shoots himself.

Geneviève Bergeron
Hélène Colgan
Nathalie Croteau
Barbara Daigneault
Anne-Marie Edward
Maud Haviernick
Barbara Maria Klueznick
Maryse Laganière
Maryse Leclair
Anne-Marie Lemay
Sonia Pelletier
Michèle Richard
Annie Saint-Arneault
Annie Turcotte

It's the worst single-day massacre in Canadian history. In response, Kim introduces a bill that allows owners of Uzis or AK-47s to keep their weapons but bans or restricts all other military-style assault rifles, creating stricter regulations for buying firearms. Bill C-17 is praised by most MPs as a great advance in public safety and becomes law two years after the Montreal Massacre.

Chapter 4

Kim Campbell, MP

1989
Kim becomes minister of state (Indian and Northern Development).

1990
Kim becomes Canada's first female justice minister.

The media dubs her the "Madonna of Politics" when she poses bare-shouldered for a portrait that becomes very controversial.

1991
Kim introduces an amendment to the criminal code for tighter gun laws.

Those two little letters after Kim's name meant a new life in Canada's capital. Kim and Howard rented a nice apartment there, and Howard soon found work as a lawyer for the **Immigration and Refugee Board**.

They were living in Ottawa for just over a month when Prime Minister Brian Mulroney asked Kim to respond to the **Speech from the Throne**. When she switched to French halfway through, he exclaimed with pleasant surprise, "She speaks French!" Then, on an evening in January 1989, Mulroney asked to meet with Kim at 7:45 at 24 Sussex Drive. It seemed strange to her that he'd ask to meet with her so early the next morning, but of course she agreed. Was she ever embarrassed when Mulroney's chief of staff called her around 9 p.m. and said the PM had been expecting her that night. He had even called the commissioner of the RCMP to see if the Mounties could find her! Nevertheless, over the phone that night, the PM invited Kim to join the government as minister of state for Indian Affairs and Northern Development (DIAND).

Kim's work that year in the DIAND taught her a great deal, but mainly that the relationship between government and native Canadians was the "worst of all possible worlds" and the aboriginal people deserved a justice that they were not getting. The issue would remain with her, even after she left the DIAND in February 1990 to become Canada's first female justice minister.

Kim wasn't the only woman from BC setting records for becoming the first woman to hold various leadership positions.

Rita Johnston became the first woman to lead a province when she became premier of BC in 1991.

Scrapper Campbell

One of Kim's first jobs as justice minister, with only two years of federal politics under her belt, was to steer proposed legislation, Bill C-43, An Act in Respect of Abortion, through Parliament.

It seemed that nearly everyone in Canada at the time was against the Bill—except the Conservative government. Many political strategists believe that Mulroney was cunning in appointing Kim, a vocal pro-choicer and feminist, to help convince Canadians to compromise on such a divisive issue. Mulroney was hugely unpopular among Canadians at the time. Was he using Kim like a pawn in a chess game, setting her up to take all the heat, so that he would get fewer negative headlines?

Regardless of Mulroney's agenda, Kim felt that the proposed legislation was better than having no federal abortion law at all. A feminist and pro-choicer, she didn't believe that this bill prevented women from getting abortions; rather, she believed it reasonably restricted them. It required abortions to be performed by a doctor or someone acting under a doctor's direction.

The media suggested Kim was compromising her pro-choice ideals to defend her government's new legislation. Pro-choice proponents called her a traitor.

Bill C-43 received the three readings required to pass in the **House of Commons**, but on February 1, 1991, the **Senate** defeated the bill.

Massacre sparks new legislation

It was the worst single-day massacre in Canadian history. On December 6, 1989, an armed and enraged man entered Montreal's École Polytechnique screaming, "Je hais les feministes." (I hate feminists.) He shot and killed 14 women and then shot himself.

After this tragedy, many groups were formed to end men's violence against women and Canadians petitioned the government for stricter gun control laws. In response, in June 1990 Kim introduced Bill C-80, which prohibited the use of all large rifles. When she got little support for that bill, she came up with a new proposal: Bill C-17. This bill allowed owners of Uzis or AK-47s to keep their weapons but banned or restricted all other military-style assault rifles and established stricter regulations regarding the purchase of firearms. Bill C-17 was praised by most MPs as a great advance in public safety and became law two years after the Montreal Massacre.

While forging her way through controversial issues in her professional life, Kim must deal with an emotional setback in her personal life.

1991

Her marriage can't weather the demands of her very public life. She and Howard separate in 1991 and divorce two years later.

Kim had been in politics now for seven years and had developed her own political style, which she began to refer to as the "politics of inclusion."

She thought it essential to consider and include the opinions of ordinary citizens—especially women—when making important political decisions; for example, consulting with women's groups on issues which were of great importance to them.

In a speech announcing her campaign, Kim explained, "If we want to change the way we do politics, we have to change people's sense of what is in fact possible."

She understood that for people to truly feel they can make a difference, they need to know "that those who are making public policy understand who [they] are."

"No means no"

Kim also began drafting a **Criminal Code** amendment concerning the amount of information that could be presented to juries about victims of sexual assault. She knew that it wasn't the victim's past behaviour that was important but rather the facts of the case. In drafting the guidelines, Kim consulted with women's groups and law associations, as well as ministry officials. No MP had ever done this before.

The new law soon became known as the "No Means No" law. It focused the public's attention on the crime of sexual assault and resulted in No Means No campaigns across university campuses in the early 1990s.

Human rights for all Canadians!

More pressure came when Justice Minister Kim Campbell began work to amend the Canadian Human Rights Act (CHRA). Kim supported several changes, including stopping discrimination based on sexual orientation (for example, whether one is heterosexual or homosexual), or political belief, eliminating mandatory retirement, and accommodating the special needs of people with disabilities, as well as people of religious and ethnic minorities. Getting agreement on the drafting of these amendments, however, proved difficult. Kim used her style of "inclusive justice" once again. And although many of the participants complained that they were given only six days' notice to prepare, fifty people were invited to present material that would be used to improve human rights for all.

But while Conservative MPs agreed with the proposed amendments dealing with mandatory retirement and people with disabilities, members of the **family caucus**, a group of MPs with highly traditional religious values, resisted all of Kim's efforts to include gay rights.

As a compromise, Kim proposed a bill that would instead protect gay people against discrimination by their employers but would not make all discrimination against gay people a crime. She felt this was a step in the right direction.

Kim says this was one of the "riskiest moments" of her career as justice minister. Church groups complimented Kim and her team for this proposal, but gay activists were infuriated. Kim was frustrated. With strong criticism from the gay community, the bill never passed its first hurdle. No similar bill was passed while Kim was in Parliament. Many critics feel that her failure to get this important human rights bill accepted by parliament damaged her image as a highly competent minister.

The "Year of the Gun": A call for new gun-control laws?

The year 2005 has been referred to in the media as the "Year of the Gun" in Toronto. It culminated in the tragic December 26 death of teenager Jane Creba, as two gangs fired at each other on downtown Yonge Street. Police reported that 107 homicides in Canada were believed to be gang related that year; 35 more than in 2004. Two-thirds of gang-related homicides involved a firearm, most often a handgun.

If you were the justice minister today, what would you propose as a step toward reducing gun crimes in Canada?

You may have plenty of time to think about that question, because some legislation take months—even years—before it is passed in Parliament and can become law. Some bills are never accepted and need to be re-introduced after several changes are made. Then there are the laws that take forever for one government to establish, but then are altered almost as soon as a new party takes over! Canada's gun-control registry is a good example of controversial legislation that took years to become law under one party, and today that law is being contested by a different political party.

Kim Campbell's Bill C-17, which became law in December 1991, was the government's first attempt to set guidelines about gun use besides a few 1978 amendments to the criminal code. However, Bill C-68, which was accepted by the Senate in 1995, remains the strictest gun-control legislation in Canadian history. This legislation created more severe penalties for crimes involving the use of guns, created the Firearms Act, and required gun owners to be licensed and registered. The legislation was introduced by Jean Chrétien's Liberals under Justice Minister Allan Rock, in part because of mounting public pressure for stricter gun laws after the 1989 murder of 14 female students at Montréal's l'École Polytechnique in Montreal.

A little over ten years later, Conservatives are attempting to change that strict legislation. In June 2006, Stephen Harper's Conservative government introduced legislation to abolish the long-gun registry, and Public Safety Minister Stockwell Day introduced a bill to amend the criminal code and Firearms Act so that owners of non-restricted rifles and shotguns don't have to register their weapons. They say the handgun registry will remain in place, as will bans on automatic and assault weapons.

Why the change? Conservative Justice Minister Vic Toews says the gun registry doesn't work to reduce gun crimes in Canada. "Police reported that, since 1997, 83% of recovered firearms used to kill were not registered," he says. In addition, it now costs over $1 billion dollars a year just to maintain the registry.

The justice minister wants the government to focus instead on punishment for gang-related gun crimes. Bill C-10, which was introduced in November 2006, would impose mandatory minimum sentences for a variety of gun- and gang-related offences.

For more information about gun control, visit our website at www.jackfruitpress.com.

1992

An elite regiment, Canadian Airbourn Regiment, is sent to help keep the peace in war-torn Somalia. But the unit is struggling due to poor rations and undisciplined soldiers. When Shidane Arone, a Somalian teenager, sneaks into the camp, he is captured by Master Corporal Clayton Matchee and Private Kyle Brown.

Arone is beaten and killed by Matchee while Brown takes photos and sixteen others ignore his cries for help. At first Canadians are told that Arone died of natural causes. But the truth comes out and the reputation of the Canadian forces is tarnished, and many believe that Kim hid the truth in order to win votes.

1992
Kim introduces an amendment to the criminal code concerning sexual assaults.

1993
She becomes minister of national defence and veterans' affairs.

Chapter 5

Don't mess with Kim —she's got tanks!

It was 1992, and it looked like Prime Minister Brian Mulroney might resign as leader of the Progressive Conservative (PC) party. All through that year, Kim's chief of staff Ray Castelli would receive regular calls from party members offering support to Kim if she decided to campaign for leadership of the Tories once Brian Mulroney stepped down. If Kim won the PC's leadership bid, not only would she become leader of the Conservative party, but the **governor general** would ask her to become prime minister.

When Parliament took a break for the summer of 1992, Kim spent many days deep in thought. Did she want the job, or did she simply like the idea of people thinking that she could be prime minister? She also worried about how becoming prime minister would change her life. Would she have to give up even more of the privacy that she loved? Would she have to give up spending time with good friends? Most importantly, would she be forced to be someone she was not?

Kim wrestled with those questions all summer, never completely finding answers for them. Her friends and family also spent hours discussing the leadership with her, and how she could raise the money required to run a campaign. At some point she made up her mind. When the opportunity came, she would reach for the top rung of the ladder that she'd been steadily climbing.

Kim and controversies

On January 3, 1993, Mulroney (who was still the PM) pulled a surprise cabinet shuffle. Kim became Canada's first female minister of defence, which also made her the first female defence minister of a **North Atlantic Treaty Organization** (NATO) country. She also became responsible for Veterans Affairs, was named to the Operations Committee, and was appointed vice-chair of the cabinet's Committee on Foreign and Defence Policy.

Kim no longer had to deal with gay rights and gun control—issues that put her in the bad books of religious and rural Tory delegates whose support she would need to become the next Tory leader—but she still found herself at the centre of two huge controversies.

First, as minister of defence, she had to justify the government's plans to purchase expensive EH-101 military helicopters. Critics said they were inappropriate now that the **world's superpowers** were no longer racing to have the greatest weapons. The second controversy involved an inquiry into the behaviour of members of the Canadian Armed Forces serving on a humanitarian mission in Somalia. Among other horrific events, two Canadian Forces members were accused of causing the death of a Somali teenager, **Shidane Arone**. The media and opposition members claimed that Kim was downplaying, perhaps even covering up, how much she knew about Arone's death to avoid a controversy that could affect her election campaign.

Happy trails

On February 24th, 1993, Mulroney finally announced his retirement. Kim immediately found herself at the centre of all kinds of positive media attention. Why? She was on the path toward becoming Canada's first female prime minister!

Kim officially announced her intention to run for leadership in March. Poll results convinced Conservative MPs that she had what it took to win the next federal election. Most of them, even the senior ones, rushed to back her. Opponents such as **Jean Charest** and Jim Edwards were practically cast aside in the shadow of her media attention. It was one of the rare times in her career when the media cheered for Kim.

The media decided to play up the angle that Kim was a woman running for leadership. They criticized her hair, her outfits, and the fact that she wore the same earrings almost daily. Some even made fun of her hot pink campaign colours.

Do you think they critiqued the male leadership contenders the same way?

Kim announced her decision to run for Conservative Party leadership in March and most Conservative MPs, even the senior ones, rushed to back her. Canadians were excited by her vibrancy and for once, the media also seemed to cheer for Kim.

1993

Sunday, June 13. Voting day. Kim is exhausted from the convention. When the results of the first ballot are announced, she has 48% of the total and her opponent, Jean Charest, has 39.

Kim's whole body feels numb as she takes her place to wait to hear the final numbers. The results are revealed and the crowd goes wild! A woman has just become prime minister for the first time in Canada! From that moment on, Kim's every move will be history in the making.

Chapter 6

In and out in a flash

1993

Kim divorces Howard Eddy.

Kim becomes the first female prime minister of Canada on June 25.

She leaves office on November 4, after the **Liberal party** wins the federal election by a landslide.

She becomes lecturer and a fellow of the Centre for Public Leadership at the John F. Kennedy School of Government in California.

Sunday, June 13, 1993 was voting day. By now, Kim was exhausted. When the results of the first ballot were announced, she had 48 per cent of the total and Charest had 39 per cent. Hearing that announcement, their opponent Jim Edwards, who had received 307 votes, walked over from his section to Kim's section and put on a Campbell button to show his support! Kim's whole body felt numb as she took her place to wait to hear the final numbers. Then her standing was announced—a win of 1,817 votes—and the crowd went wild!

A woman had just become prime minister for the first time in Canada! From that moment on, every move Kim made would be history in the making.

The day after Kim was elected leader of the Progressive Conservative party, she met with Brian Mulroney at **24 Sussex Drive** to settle the date for her swearing-in as Canada's prime minister. Something revealing happened when the PM led Kim to the front of the house to speak with the press. In saying farewell, Mulroney gave her a little hug. While the gesture was a kind one, would Mulroney have shown public affection to her in that way had she been a man? Kim didn't think so. Plus, she was concerned, as she did not want to appear to be too friendly with the very unpopular Mulroney. She wanted Canadians to see that the old leader was gone, and that she was very different.

Scandals

Kim was mixed up in several scandals over the years, each of which was reported in the press. She was criticized for:

1. Photograph of her with bare shoulders
2. Shidane Arone and "cover up" over his death in Somalia
3. Statement: elections no place to discuss serious issues
4. Statement: unemployment not going to improve for 10 years
5. Statement: reporters need hearing aids (said in frustration for other misquotes but offends hearing impaired voters)
4. Ad showing deformity of Chretien's mouth

Canada's love afair with Kim begins . . .

Over the summer, Kim received the highest approval rating for a prime minister in 30 years. The media seemed to be giving her a fresh start. Canadians saw her as a welcome change.

During her four months as prime minister, Kim had one major achievement: a massive reorganization of government departments, the most radical reorganization since **Confederation**. She created the Department of Canadian Heritage and the Department of Human Resources. She expanded, renamed, and amalgamated several other departments. She also downsized her cabinet to twenty-five people. This downsizing proved to be a popular move with most Canadians who appreciated that Kim was living up to her leadership campaign promises.

. . . and ends soon after

In September, Kim announced that there would be a federal election on October 25. Would she be re-elected as PM?

Her troubles began. Voters expected her to reaffirm her commitment to keep the government's military helicopters while reducing research and development costs. Instead, she went along with the Defence Department and cut seven aircrafts. In her campaign speeches, she was promising jobs and greater opportunity should she be re-elected. When asked how long the public would have to wait before the unemployment rate was below 10%, Kim replied honestly, saying it might be "two, three, or four years," which meant 1997 at the latest. Her opponent, Liberal Leader **Jean Chrétien**, "spun" these words to suggest that Kim had said there would be no reduction in unemployment until 2000. For job-hungry Canadians, this was simply too long to wait for an improvement!

In stepped the media—kicking her when she was down. A huge media debate began over whether her remarks were actually a gaffe or a new form of political integrity. Chrétien's distortion of what she had said made the debate even more complicated.

Kim's popularity had evaporated. Canadians polled during the campaign didn't believe she could relate to them and found her overly condescending—brash even. Her campaign continued to slide downhill when the media misinterpreted her comment that an election was the "worst possible time" to discuss a complete overhaul of Canada's social policies in great detail. She meant that the forty-seven days allotted to an election campaign wasn't enough time to tackle those significant issues; the media reports translated her comment as "an election is no time to discuss serious issues."

Honesty and spin in the spotlight

Can public figures ever be completely honest? If they speak the complete truth without spinning their statements, do they risk their popularity and therefore their careers? And what exactly does it mean to "spin" a statement? According to the dictionary it means to provide an interpretation of an event or statement in such a way as to sway public opinion. A "spin doctor" is someone who works to ensure that a public figure's words and deeds are presented positively in the media.

For example think of a person described as "stubborn" — suggests that the person is difficult to work with, unreasonable even. But what if the same person is described as "determined" instead? It still means that the person is not going to change their mind easily, but by looking at the characteristic in a different way you can change the way a person's actions are perceived from negative to positive! Easy, eh?

Honest politicians don't seem to get very far. Kim Campbell often spoke what she felt was the truth to the public and it got her in hot water almost every time. When asked how long Canadians would have to wait before unemployment dipped below double digits (it was over 10 percent) she honestly replied that "it may be two, three, or four year before the unemployment rate lowered". That may have been true but as her campaign staff reminded her, "you have to feed people hope". And that is exactly what her political opponent, Liberal Leader Jean Chrétien did: promising that his party would be the one to create jobs for Canadians.

There are many ways to alter your message so that what comes out makes people like you more and also so it makes headline news. For instance, you can "skirt" the issues such as Chrétien did, by saying his party would get Canadians working without actually answering the question that sunk Kim.

Another way to "spin the truth" is to present the facts selectively, as one reporter did when Kim suggested that the 47 days allowed for an election are not enough time to really describe and come to grips with a complete change of all of Canada's social policies. As Kim told the reporter, such changes are simply too complex. The reporter instead quoted Kim as saying that "an election is not time to discuss serious issues". A bit different from her actual message, don't you think?

William Lyon Mackenzie King was Canada's most successful prime minister. He won election after election and stayed in power for a record 21 years. He was very good at saying things in such a way that opposing sides both believed he was on their side! For instance, during World War II, his message to Canadians was "Conscription if necessary but not necessarily conscription". This issue was dividing the country; King even feared there could be civil war as the majority of English-Canadians were for conscription while most French Canadians were against it. By carefully crafting his message, he got the English to believe he was promising there would be conscription while the French felt assured that there would not be conscription! Clever, eh?

For more information about spin, visit our website at www.jackfruitpress.com.

Results of the 1993 election:

Kim loses and Chrétien becomes Canada's 20th prime minister

Population:	27,296,859	
Eligible voters:	19,906,796	
Valid votes cast:	13,667,671	

How the numbers stacked up:

Party	# votes	# seats
PC	2,186,422	2
Liberal	5,647,952	177
NDP	939,575	9
Reform	2,559,245	52
BQ	1,846,024	54
Other	488,453	1
Total	13,667,671	295

Issues: economic recession
constitutional reform

When Liberal MP **Sheila Copps** called Kim "Brian Mulroney in a skirt," anti-Conservative activists agreed, claiming Kim was displaying the attitudes and political stances of her much-despised predecessor. They gathered at her campaign stops, chanting, "Kim, Kim, you're just like him!"

Devastation

Then a set of television ads for Kim's campaign turned the public almost completely against her. The ads made fun of Jean Chrétien's facial deformity, showing a photo of his lopsided grin and commenting, "Is this a prime minister? Why doesn't he answer the questions he's asked? Doesn't he understand the questions? Or the answer? Think twice." Kim didn't see the ads until after they aired and was mortified! She described them as both "stupid and offensive," but it was too late. Though the ads were quickly pulled off the air, the Liberals grabbed the opportunity to refer to them with their own set of TV ads, reminding the public of the low blow the other team had taken. "It was now clear to everybody that we couldn't win," Kim says.

In the end, the Progressive Conservatives were completely devastated by the Liberals, failing to gain the twelve seats required for official party status. Kim even lost her own seat.

"Consider yourselves hugged"

Despite her overwhelming disappointment, Kim managed to stay spunky on election night. In Kim's concession speech, her public acceptance of her defeat, she consoled her party members by promising the Conservative party would have their moment in the sun again after a process of "renewal and rebuilding." She was right, but it would take over a decade, until 2006, for Stephen Harper's Conservatives to win the federal election and dethrone the Liberals!

With her speech nearing its end, Kim couldn't face walking amongst that ballroom full of 200 dejected party members. Instead, she simply closed with one of her father's expressions, "Consider yourselves hugged," and slipped away from the crowd.

After a short 132 days in power, Kim Campbell was PM no more.

The Progressive Conservatives are demolished in the election, failing to gain the twelve seats needed for official party status. Kim even loses her own seat. In her concession speech, she consoles her party with promises of rebuilding and renewing.

Distribution of seats in Federal Parliament after the 1988 election

- Progressive Conservatives
- Liberals
- New Democrats

Distribution of seats in Federal Parliament after the 1993 election

- Progressive Conservatives
- Liberals
- New Democrats
- Reform
- Bloc Québécois

"Consider yourselves hugged."

With her speech nearing its end, Kim can't face walking amongst that ballroom full of 200 dejected party members. Instead, she simply closes with one of her father's expressions, "Consider yourselves hugged," and slips away from the crowd.

TD 07

After staying out of the spotlight for two years, Kim finds herself missing the interactions she'd once enjoyed with the Canadian public.

CONSULATE GENERAL OF CANADA IN LOS ANGELES

CONSULAT GÉNÉRAL DU CANADA À LOS ANGELES

KIM CAMPBELL
CONSUL GENERAL

GATE
C29

WORLD TRAVELLER

CAMPBELL/KIM M
BA   99   31JAN

BOARDING P

COUNCIL OF
Women World Leaders

The Right Honourable
Kim Campbell PC, QC, LL.

Harvard University

KIM C
Departm

ON AIR

THE RIGH
KIM CA

- Club of Madrid Speech
- "Noah's arc" dress rehearsal
Title for my b

So, for five weeks in the summer of 1995, she returns to the public eye as a talk-show host for one of Vancouver's most popular private radio stations, CKNW. She seems a bit nervous at first but quickly gets the hang of it. Kim enjoys hosting and interviewing for radio so much that she dabbles in it again in May of 1996—this time for the British Broadcasting Corporation (BBC).

d saw under the sun,
's not to the swift,
o the strong, neither
e wise, nor yet
f understanding, nor
favour to men of skill; but
time and chance happeneth to them all.

Ecclesiastes 9:11

title of
my book?

CLUB DE MADRID

Chapter 7

Professor and Women's Advocate

Imagine a small piece of white paper with Kim Campbell's name on it, taped to the wall beside a door.

By 1994, this was as fancy as it got when it came to announcing the office of Canada's first female former prime minister. But Kim was too busy to care. She spent the early part of 1994 in the United States at Harvard University's Institute of Politics, teaching a study group comparative Canadian and American political processes. She also worked on her political memoir (*Time and Chance*), spoke at several conferences across the United States, and joined Margaret Thatcher and other internationally famous people at a conference in Turkey concerning cultural identity and politics.

In the fall of 1994, Kim returned to Harvard on a $10,000 US fellowship. Her research paper was on a topic she was all too familiar with: the relationship between the media and the political process. Its special focus? The cynicism and mistrust between the media and politicians.

On the air

After staying out of the spotlight for two years, Kim found herself missing the dialogue she had once enjoyed with the Canadian public. So, for five weeks in the summer of 1995, she returned to the public eye as a talk-show host for one of Vancouver's most popular private radio stations, CKNW. She "seemed a bit nervous at first but quickly got the hang of it," said CBC's Peter Mansbridge about Kim's

1996
Kim is appointed Canadian consul general in Los Angeles by Prime Minister Jean Chrétien.

She publishes her memoirs, *Time and Chance*.

1997
Kim begins a common-law marriage with Hershey Felder.

1999
Kim becomes chair of the Council of Women World Leaders.

2002
Kim is a founding member and vice-president of the Club of Madrid.

2003
Kim becomes president of the International Women's Forum.

2004
Kim becomes secretary general of the Club of Madrid.

Her official portrait is unveiled for the parliamentary prime ministers' gallery.

2007
Kim is one of four former prime ministers who judge candidates on television series "The Next Great Prime Minister".

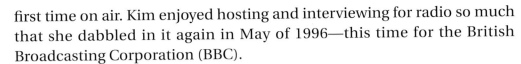

first time on air. Kim enjoyed hosting and interviewing for radio so much that she dabbled in it again in May of 1996—this time for the British Broadcasting Corporation (BBC).

Later that same year, Kim was appointed Canadian **consul general** in Los Angeles by Prime Minister Jean Chrétien. As a diplomat, it was her job to represent Canadians, a task she enjoyed a great deal. "One of the pleasures of being a diplomat was the opportunity to talk about who [Canadians] really are. There are many things about us that Americans don't know."

Kim acted like "a magnet for Canadians," according to Laura Liswood, the creator of the Council for Women World Leaders. "It's amazing. Canadians come right up to her because she carries herself in an approachable way. That's part of her appeal."

Speaking out

Kim was a diplomat until 2000, but held other appointments at the same time. From 2000 to 2003 she was chair of the Council of Women World Leaders, a network of current and former female heads of state and government, and in 2002 she became a founding member and vice-president of the **Club of Madrid**, an independent organization with the goal of contributing to strengthening democracy in the world. She took on the role of secretary general for the Club in 2004.

Kim remains a lecturer in public policy at the Kennedy School of Government at Harvard University and speaks at conferences around the world on her two main concerns: the advancement of women and the advancement of **democracy**. "I don't think it hurts to have a group of women who are sitting at a table, to have a couple of old female prime ministers and presidents hanging around, reminding people that women have a right to be at the table and have something to offer," she has said about her place on the Council of Women World Leaders.

Kim's official portrait as prime minister was unveiled in 2004 and included a playful nod to her infamous naked-shoulder photograph: the legal robes that she held up in that photo are draped over her armchair. After the hanging of the portrait in the House of Commons, she joked that **Paul Martin**, who was prime minister at the time, should get going on his portrait early, because by the time she was ready to have hers painted, she was "ten years older and a lot fatter" than when she was prime minister!

Kim said it was hard being Canada's first lady on the hill—Parliament Hill, that is.

She said: "If I'd known then what I know now, I might have been scared away from running. Or at least I might have been more astute in my expectations, because it all kind of puzzled me, why no one was interested in my record.

And I realized that when you're a woman, your accomplishments don't stick to you. Women are not seen as belonging as leaders; their success is really seen as a kind of a fluke."

Women in power

The first woman prime minister ever to be elected was Sirimavo Bandaranaike in 1960. She declared her country a republic in 1972, changing its name from Ceylon to Sri Lanka.

Some countries still don't have any women in parliament. In 2000, only 13% of the world's pembers of parliament were women. At that time, Sweden had the highest percentage of women in parliament: 42.7% compared to the United Kingdom, with 18.4%, and Ethiopia, with 2%.

Not only is it difficult to attain these positions as a woman, but, while a woman is climbing to the top, and once she's arrived, she's faced with the challenge of gender bias in the media. Kim Campbell researched the issue of gender bias in political races, and in doing so, reviewed her own re-election campaign. She learned that the media "repeatedly acknowledged" that she was getting unfair treatment, but reporters rarely tried to figure out why. She argues that reporters were reacting to "unconscious ideals and expectations of women," ones they didn't even know they had; ideas likely reinforced since they were children.

What would it take to get more women in positions of power today? Perhaps we need less women being created as stereotypical characters in movies and fairy tales, and more women actually taking on powerful positions in the world, acting as role models to young women. Laura Liswood, secretary general of the **Council of Women World Leaders** (of which Kim Campbell is the chair emerita) has said that,

"Women have not been socialized to see themselves as leaders. You think about the major fairy tales and stories and myths and legends that young girls grow up with . . . in the United States, it's Cinderella. She's waiting for her prince to come and rescue her. He's the hero, he's the leader, and she's sitting at home talking to the mice, so there's not a sense that she can be a leader. She should be a leader. But the young girl doesn't grow up seeing that."

There are a few countries where the tables are turned.

In Iceland, for example, female president Vigdis Finnbogadottir discovered that most young girls 8 years old and younger, thought that only a woman could be president of Iceland! The boys actually asked if they were allowed to become president. "That's how you see what can be in the world," explained Liswood, "It's what's out there for you."

What's "out there" in terms of strong role models for young women could change dramatically in the next five or so years. As Kim Campbell recently said, "Women cannot rely on [the power of their] office alone for people to follow their vision. It's extremely important for women leaders to keep pushing the envelope because things are beginning to change." Someone who's almost always pushing the edge of the envelope is Senator Hilary Rodham Clinton, who in late 2006 was hinting that she'd seek nomination as a democratic candidate in the 2008 presidential bid.

In what ways do you think our world will change if she becomes the first female president of the United States?

For more information about this topic, visit our website at www.jackfruitpress.com.

Kim Campbell: Making

Kim Campbell had a lonely childhood and a shaky climb to the top of the political ladder. It wasn't easy being a woman playing a man's game, fielding frequent attacks from the media. Then, when she finally reached the top rung of that ladder and became prime minister, her prize "slipped through [her] fingers." She fell almost immediately. Kim was prime minister for only 132 days.

Yet, during her climb, Kim led Canada into a series of important firsts: first female minister of justice and attorney general, first female minister of national defence, first woman elected as leader of the Progressive Conservative party, first female Canadian prime minister and first prime minister, from British Columbia.

As justice minister, she left one important legacy: Canada's "No Means No" law, with its catch phrase now firmly entrenched in our society and improved protection for victims of sexual assault in our laws.

the best of a bad situation

As prime minister, she reorganized Parliament for the 1990s, radically cutting back the number of cabinet committees from eleven to five. That part of her legacy lasted a decade.

Kim Campbell has been prime minister, a professor, and a defender of women's rights and democracy. She jokes that she still hasn't decided what she wants to do when she grows up. But for Kim, politics was her best job. She once said: "I think, of all the things in my life, it was the thing I did best. Certainly I made lots of mistakes and put my foot in it, but I'm very good at seeing the connections between ideas and interests that bring people together, and that's a very useful skill. I really loved being in politics. It gave me an enormous amount of satisfaction."

Kim will always have a place in Canada's history books, but she feels the most pride in having "changed the sense of what is possible for many young women and girls in Canada."

Being an advocate for positive change isn't easy. But Kim's example shows that if you work hard and take a stand, you can sometimes change what seems impossible to change!

Timeline: The life and times of Kim Campbell

YEAR	KIM'S LIFE	EVENTS IN CANADA AND THE WORLD
1947	Avril Phaedra Douglas Campbell is born March 10 in Port Alberni, BC; the family moves to Vancouver soon after.	Canadian Citizenship Act is passed. The Dead Sea scrolls are found in a cave at Qumran, on the shore of the Dead Sea. India and Pakistan gain independence from Great Britain.
1959	Avril's mother, Lissa, leaves the family; she changes her name to Kim.	Queen Elizabeth II tours Canada. The development of the Avro Arrow CF-105 supersonic, all-weather interceptor jet aircraft is cancelled. The St. Lawrence Seaway opens to commercial traffic. Georges Vanier is appointed the first French-Canadian governor general. Fidel Castro becomes premier and dictator of Cuba.
1967	Kim enrolls at the University of British Columbia and majors in political science.	Canada celebrates the 100th anniversary of Confederation. The World Exposition takes place in Montreal. French president Charles de Gaulle visits Montreal and exclaims *"Vive le Québec libre"* (Long live free Quebec). The Biafran crisis erupts in Nigeria; the Republic of Biafra demands complete independence from Nigeria. The Six Day War takes place between Israel and Egypt, Jordan, and Syria. Fifty thousand people demonstrate in Washington, DC, against the Vietnam War.
1969	Kim graduates with a BA in political science from the University of British Columbia.	Parliament and federal institutions are made officially bilingual when the Official Languages Act becomes law. New Brunswick becomes first province to be officially bilingual. US astronaut Neil Armstrong becomes the first person to walk on the moon.
1970	Kim begins a doctorate at the London School of Economics in Soviet government.	Front de liberation du Québec (FLQ) terrorists kidnap two officials. The War Measures Act is passed, suspending civil liberties.
1972	Kim marries Nathan Divinsky.	Muriel McQueen Fergusson is appointed the first female speaker of the Senate.
1973	Kim leaves the London School of Economics with her thesis unfinished.	
1975	Kim begins lecturing part-time at the University of British Columbia.	Toronto's CN Tower becomes the world's tallest freestanding structure. Wage and price controls are implemented (1975–1978).
1977		Bill 101 is passed in Quebec. Canadian road signs are changed to show distances and speed limits in metric.
1979	Kim begins lecturing at the Vancouver Community College (to 1981).	Joseph Clark becomes the 16th prime minister of Canada. Margaret Thatcher becomes the first female prime minister of Great Britain.
1980	Kim begins studying law at UBC. She is elected to be a trustee of the Vancouver School Board (to 1984).	Pierre Trudeau is elected to his second term as prime minister. The Quebec referendum on sovereignty is held; the *non* vote wins. Jeanne Sauvé is appointed the first female speaker of the House of Commons. Terry Fox's Marathon of Hope begins (April 12–September 2). "O Canada" becomes the official national anthem of Canada.

More on the life and times of Kim Campbell

YEAR	KIM'S LIFE	EVENTS IN CANADA AND THE WORLD
1983	Kim is called to the Bar of BC. She divorces Nathan Divinsky. Kim becomes chair of the Vancouver School Board.	Bertha Wilson is appointed Canada's first female Supreme Court justice. Jeanne Sauvé is appointed the first female governor general. The ARPANET officially changes to use the Internet Protocol, creating the Internet. Sally Ride becomes first US female in space on the Space Shuttle *Challenger*.
1984	Kim runs as a Social Credit (Socred) candidate in the BC provincial election and loses. She becomes vice-chair of the Vancouver School Board.	John Napier Turner becomes the 17th prime minister of Canada. Brian Mulroney becomes the 18th prime minister of Canada. Marc Garneau becomes the first Canadian to go into outer space. Bhopal disaster occurs in Bhopal, India; a chemical leak from a pesticide plant kills more than 2,000 people outright and injures anywhere from 150,000 to 600,000 others in one of the worst industrial disasters in history.
1985	Kim becomes director of the Office of the Premier of BC, William Bennett.	Air India flight 182, from Toronto, is blown up over the Atlantic Ocean killing 329 passengers; 280 Canadians are killed. Amendments are made to the Indian Act to include the right of First Nations peoples to self-government.
1986	Kim runs for leader of the BC Socreds after William Bennett resigns, but loses to Bill Vander Zalm. She wins a seat in provincial legislature as a Socred member. Kim marries Howard Eddy.	The World Exposition is held in Vancouver, BC. Canada endorses sanctions against the South African apartheid government. Canada is honoured by the United Nations for providing refuge to refugees. Space Shuttle *Challenger* disintegrates 73 seconds after launch, killing all seven astronauts on board. IBM unveils the PC Convertible, its first laptop computer. In Ukraine, one of the reactors at the Chernobyl nuclear plant explodes, creating the world's worst nuclear disaster. Iran-Contra Affair occurs: the United States had been selling weapons to Iran in secret then illegally diverting the money to anti-communist Contra rebels in Nicaragua.
1988	Kim runs and wins a seat in the House of Commons as a member of the Progressive Conservative Party for Vancouver Centre.	Calgary hosts 1988 Winter Olympics. The Emergencies Act replaces War Measures Act. Government announces a settlement and a formal apology for the treatment of Japanese-Canadians during World War II. The French language sign law of Quebec is reinstated. After more than eight years of fighting, the Russian Army begins its withdrawal from Afghanistan. A ceasefire begins in the Iran-Iraq war. The Netherlands becomes the second country to get connected to the Internet.
1989	Kim becomes minister of state for Indian and Northern Development.	The Canada-US Free Trade Agreement (FTA) comes into effect. The one-dollar bill is replaced with the one-dollar coin commonly known as the "loonie". A massacre occurs at L'école polytechnique in Montreal. George Herbert Walker Bush is sworn in as president of the US. The first of 24 satellites of the Global Positioning System (GPS) is placed into orbit. Tiananmen Square student protests lead to a massacre in Beijing, China. The Berlin Wall falls in Germany.

Still more on the life and times of Kim Campbell

YEAR	KIM'S LIFE	EVENTS IN CANADA AND THE WORLD
1990	Kim becomes Canada's first female minister of justice.	The Oka crisis takes place in Quebec: Mohawks from the Kanesatake reserve barricade the road to the city of Oka to protest plans to expand a golf course onto their land. Elijah Harper refuses to accept the Meech Lake Accord in the Manitoba legislature: the accord guarantees no rights to First Nations peoples. Manitoba does not accept the Accord, which cancels its acceptance into the Canadian Constitution. The Bloc Québecois Party forms.
1991	Kim introduces an amendment to the Criminal Code for more restrictive gun laws.	Canadian forces enter the Gulf War against Iraq. Julius Alexander Isaac becomes the first Black Chief Justice. Rita Johnston of BC becomes the first female provincial premier. The Gulf War ends with liberation of Kuwait. The Soviet Union collapses as countries declare independence.
1992	Kim introduces an amendment to the Criminal Code concerning sexual assaults.	Roberta Bondar becomes the first Canadian woman to travel into space. The Toronto Blue Jays win the World Series. The Charlottetown Accord is rejected in a referendum. Members of the Canadian Airborne Regiment are sent to Somalia on a peacekeeping mission. US military forces invade Somalia.
1993	Kim divorces Howard Eddy. She becomes Minister of National Defence, and Veterans Affairs. Kim becomes the first female and the 19th prime minister of Canada on June 25, 1993– Nov. 4, 1993. She becomes lecturer and a Fellow of the Centre for Public Leadership at Harvard University.	Shidane Arone, a Somali youth, is beaten to death by members of the Canadian Airborne Regiment. The Nunavut Land Claims Agreement Act and the Nunavut Act are passed. Jean Chrétien becomes the 20th prime minister of Canada (1993–2003). Czechoslovakia divides with the establishment of independent Slovakia and the Czech Republic. Bill Clinton is sworn in as president of the US.
1994		The North Atlantic Free Trade Agreement (NAFTA) between Canada, US, and Mexico comes into effect. The Channel Tunnel, which took 15,000 workers over seven years to complete, opens between England and France. Boris Yeltsin orders troops into Chechnya.
1995		The Airborne Regiment is disbanded due to the Somali Affair in 1993. A plebiscite is held by the Cree of Quebec: a huge majority are in favour of remaining as part of Canada. A referendum on separation from Canada is held in Quebec: the "no" vote wins again by a slim margin. Canadian peacekeepers are sent to Bosnia. For the first time in 26 years, no British soldiers patrol the streets of Belfast, Northern Ireland. Bosnian Serbs march into Srebrenica and force UN Dutch peacekeepers to leave: a massacre follows.
1996	Kim is appointed Canadian Consul General in Los Angeles. She publishes her political memoirs *Time and Chance*	Dolly the sheep, the first mammal to be successfully cloned from an adult cell, is born.
1997	Kim begins a common-law marriage with Hershey Felder.	Jacques Villeneuve becomes the first Canadian to receive a world car racing title. NASA's *Pathfinder* space probe lands on the surface of Mars. Princess Diana and Dodi Fayed die following a car crash in Paris.

Even more on the life and times of Kim Campbell

YEAR	KIM'S LIFE	EVENTS IN CANADA AND THE WORLD
1998		Prime Minister Jean Chrétien makes an official visit to Cuba. The Supreme Court rules that Quebec cannot legally separate from Canada without the approval of the federal government. The value of the Canadian dollar drops to 64.02 US cents on August 28. Canada takes a seat on the United Nations Security Council. Google Inc. is founded.
1999	She becomes chair of the Council of Women World Leaders (CWWL) (to 2003).	Nunavut, Canada's third territory, is formed. Julie Payette becomes first Canadian to board International Space Station. The world population surpasses 6 billion.
2000		Clarity Bill is passed: the guideline for ensuring that the referendum question on the separation of Quebec must be clearly worded and supported by a clear majority. The Reform Party is dissolved and replaced with the Canadian Alliance. Former Prime Minister Pierre Elliot Trudeau dies.
2001		Canada becomes the first country in the world to legalize medicinal marijuana. George Walker Bush is sworn in as president of the USA. An estimated 3,000 people are killed in the September 11, 2001 terrorist attack on the World Trade Center in New York City, the Pentagon in Arlington, Virginia, and rural Pennsylvania. American, Australian, and British troops invade Afghanistan. Canadian troops are committed to provide military contribution to operations in Afghanistan.
2002	Kim becomes a founding member and vice president of the Club of Madrid.	Stem cell research using human embryos is approved. Quebec becomes the first province to grant full parental rights to homosexual couples. Pope John Paul II visits Toronto for World Youth Day. Queen Elizabeth II tours Canada to mark her Golden Jubilee. Canada signs the Kyoto Protocol, promising to reduce greenhouse gases. Queen Elizabeth II celebrates the Golden Jubilee (50th anniversary) of her reign.
2003	Kim becomes president of the International Women's Forum.	Paul Martin becomes the 21st prime minister of Canada (December 12). An outbreak of Severe Acute Respiratory Syndrome (SARS) hits Toronto. Mad-cow disease (bovine spongiform encephalopathy) is discovered in a northern Alberta farm, threatening the beef industry. The Space Shuttle Columbia disintegrates over Texas upon reentry, killing all seven astronauts on board. The Iraq War begins: land troops from the USA, United Kingdom, Australia and Poland invade Iraq.
2004	Kim becomes the Secretary General of the Club of Madrid. Her official portrait is unveiled for the parliamentary Prime Minister's gallery.	Tsunami tidal waves sweep across much of the coastlines of Sri Lanka, India, Bangladesh, the Maldives, Burma, Thailand, Malaysia and Indonesia killing at least 290,000 people from South Asia to as far as Somalia in Africa.
2007	Kim is one of four former prime ministers who judge candidates on television series "The Next Great Prime Minister".	32 students at Virginia Polytechnic Institute and State University are shot dead by a fellow student. Live Earth concerts take place on July 7 in 11 venues around the world to kick off a 3-year campaign to reduce global warming and encourage environmentally-sustainable living.

Glossary: words and facts you might want to know

Arone, Shidane (1977?–1993): a 16-year-old Somali who was beaten and tortured to death by Canadian soldiers on March 16, 1993 in Belet Huen, Somalia. A year later, on March 16, 1994, Private Elvin Kyle Brown was sentenced to 5 years in jail for Arone's death.

Bennett, William Richards (Bill) (1932–): leader of the Social Credit Party in 1973 and the premier of British Columbia from 1975 to 1986.

boarding school: a school where students live and go to class. They may return to their own homes during holidays. Depending on the boarding school, some pupils may attend just during the day.

Charest, Jean (1958–): premier of Quebec since 2003 and leader of the of Quebec Liberal Party since 1998. A lawyer born in Quebec, Jean began his political career as an MP for the Progressive Conservative (PC) Party of Canada. He served as minister of several government departments during Brian Mulroney's term as prime minister. He ran unsuccessfully against Kim Campbell for leadership of the PC party in 1993. When she resigned as leader later that year, Jean was appointed to fill the position. In 1998, he responded to public and political pressure to switch to Quebec provincial politics.

Chrétien, Joseph Jacques Jean (1934–): 20th prime minister of Canada (1993–2003). A lawyer from Quebec, he entered politics in 1963 as a Liberal party MP. He is the only prime minister in Canada to be elected to three majority governments in a row.

Club of Madrid: an association that promotes democracy around the world. The group includes former prime ministers, presidents, and other heads of government who have experience running democratic governments. The members try to help countries that are attempting to adopt a democratic form of politics.

Confederation: on July 1, 1867, the formation of the Dominion of Canada from the union of the British North American colonies of New Brunswick, Nova Scotia and the Province of Canada (Lower Canada and Upper Canada). Manitoba and the Northwest Territories joined in 1870, British Columbia in 1871, Prince Edward Island in 1873, and Newfoundland in 1949.

consul general: the person who is head of an office, or consulate general, that represents a country in a foreign country. This person is lower in rank than an ambassador or high commissioner, who are a nation's main representative in a foreign country. The consul general and staff members assist Canadians living in the area, help people migrate to Canada, and promote trade with and business investment in Canada.

Copps, Sheila (1952–): in 1993, first woman to be named deputy prime minister. After working as a newspaper journalist, she entered politics in 1981. She has held the Cabinet positions of Minister of the Environment and Minister of Heritage. She ran twice for the leadership of the Liberal Party, in 1990 and 2003. She left politics in 2004 when the boundaries of her riding were distributed and she lost the nomination for Liberal party candidate in the new riding.

Council of Women World Leaders: founded in 1998, a global association of current and former female presidents and prime ministers. Its mission is to improve the quality of life of women around the world by promoting democracy, assisting women reach high levels in government, and increasing their visibility as they attain leadership positions.

Criminal Code: the set of government laws that outlines Canada's criminal offenses and the maximum and minimum punishments that courts can impose upon offenders when those crimes are committed. It was first enacted in 1892. The code has been revised several times including 1955 and 1985.

de Beauvoir, Simone (1908–1986): a French author and philosopher who developed the theory of modern feminism. In one of her most famous books, *The Second Sex*, she looked at the historical oppression of women and encouraged them to take responsibility for themselves and the world.

democracy: a kind of government in which the citizens of the country hold power. The people either vote for measures directly or they vote in representatives who vote for them.

Divinsky, Nathan Joseph (1925–): although known as Kim Campbell's husband from 1972–1983, Nathan Divinsky was also a mathematics professor and a chess master.

Expo '86: the international exposition, or large show, held in Vancouver, BC from May 2 to October 13, 1986. The theme was transportation and communication. Over 20 million visitors came to see ceremonies of culture and stunning displays of architecture and multi media exhibits.

More words and facts you might want to know

family caucus: members of Parliament who have a traditional set of beliefs that are focused on their views of families. For example, they are opposed to abortion, homosexuality, and same sex marriage.

fellowship: money that is given to someone by a university or other group to pay for that person to do advanced research on a subject.

feminist: a male or female who supports the idea that women deserve the same rights as men. In the past, many believed that women were supposed to cook, clean, and look after children. Feminists have helped made it possible for women to do many of the jobs that were traditionally considered men's work.

First Nations peoples: the descendants of the first inhabitants of North America. The Constitution recognizes three separate groups of aboriginal people: Indians, Métis, and Inuit. Each group has unique heritages, languages, cultural practises, and spiritual beliefs.

Friedan, Betty (1921–2006): American feminist, activist, and writer who studied the role of women in society.

governor general: the representative of the king or queen in Canada who provides Royal Assent necessary for all laws passed by Parliament. The governor general is a figurehead who only performs symbolic formal, ceremonial, and cultural duties, and whose job is to encourage Canadian excellence, identity, unity and leadership. Governor generals are Canadian citizens appointed for terms of approximately 5 years. During their term, they live and work in the official residence of Rideau Hall in Ottawa, parts of which are open to the public as a historic site, art gallery, and educational centre.

Harper, Stephen Joseph (1959–): Canada's 22nd prime minister, beginning in 2006. He was born in Toronto and moved to Alberta where he worked in the oil industry and later studied economics. A former member of the Progressive Conservative (PC) Party of Canada, he later took part in the formation of the Reform Party. From the Reform Party was born the Canadian Alliance, which Stephen led from 2002 until its merging with the PC party in 2004. As leader of the new Conservative Party, he won the election in January 2006 and sworn in as prime minister in February.

House of Commons: the lower house of Parliament. It consists of a Speaker, the prime minister and his Cabinet, members of the governing party, members of the opposition parties, and sometimes a few independent members (elected members who do not belong to an official party). The members of the House (called Members of Parliament or MPs) are elected in constituency elections or by-elections by the Canadian people. The House (often incorrectly referred to as Parliament) is important because it is where all new laws start.

human resources and labour department: created in 1993 by merging several existing government departments together. Its purpose was to improve the quality of life of workers and immigrants to Canada. Its current name is Human Resources and Social Development Canada.

Immigration and Refugee Board: a special court that is responsible for making decisions about individual immigration and refugee cases in Canada. It does this by applying the federal immigration and refugee acts that are passed by Parliament.

international relations: the study of world issues and how governments and non-government groups interact with each other.

Liberal Party of Canada: political party that adopted its name after Confederation in 1867. It was formed from the union of the pre-Confederation Reform Party (of shat is now Ontario) and *le Parti rouge* (in present-day Quebec).

Martin, Paul Edgar Philippe Jr. (1938–): 21st prime minister of Canada (2003–2006). Prior to entering politics, Paul was a business executive in Quebec firms. His father Paul Martin Sr. had been a Cabinet minister and candidate for the leadership of the Liberal party.

member of Parliament (MP): politician who is elected to sit in the House of Commons. During a general election, the country is divided up into ridings (or, constituencies). The voters in each riding elect one candidate to represent them in the government as their MP.

member of the Legislative Assembly (MLA): elected politician who represents the people in the provincial and territorial governments. Provinces that use other terms for their representatives at the provincial level are: Ontario (MPP, member of provincial Parliament), Newfoundland (MHA, member of the House of Assembly), and Quebec (MNA, member of the National Assembly, or députés).

More words and facts you might want to know

Mulroney, Martin Brian (1939–): 18th prime minister of Canada (1984–1993). Born in Quebec to Irish immigrants, he trained as a lawyer. He specialized in labour negotiations and eventually became president of a mining company. Without ever having run for office, Brian became leader of the Progressive Conservative (PC) Party in 1983. In 1984 he led the PC Party to win the most seats (211) in Canadian history.

New Democratic Party (NDP): founded in 1961, a national political party that was created when the Co-operative Commonwealth Federation (CCF) merged with unions within the Canadian Labour Congress. The CCF wanted to get better results in elections; the unions wanted an official way to become involved in politics. While it has yet to be in power federally, the NDP has formed the governments of Ontario, British Columbia, Yukon, Saskatchewan, and Manitoba.

North Atlantic Treaty Organization (NATO): since 1949, a group of countries that have agreed to defend each other militarily. Canada, the United States, Great Britain, and the countries of western Europe were united in order to prevent the spread of communism and the expansion of the Soviet Union.

nuns: women who devote themselves to a religious life. Some are teachers, nurses, or those who have left mainstream society to live a life of prayer in a monastery or convent. The term "nun" is used by Roman Catholics, Eastern Christians, Anglicans, Jains, Lutherans, and Buddhists. A male nun is called a monk.

Parliament: the governor general (as the Queen's representative), the Senate and the House of Commons together make up Canada's Parliament. Parliament makes laws that apply across the country.

Parliament Hill: in Ottawa, Ontario. It is the site of Canada's federal government buildings. The House of Commons, the Senate, the offices of many Members of Parliament, and committee rooms are housed here. It is a complex of buildings that sits above the Ottawa River. Construction began in 1859 and it was officially opened in 1866. It was destroyed by a fire and rebuilt in 1916.

Progressive Conservative (PC) party: the name of the Conservative Party of Canada following its union with some members of the farm-focused Progressive Party in 1942. The Conservative Party began in 1854 when politicians from Upper and Lower Canada joined to form a coalition government of the Province of Canada. Sir John A. Macdonald was its first leader. In 2004, the party merged with the Canadian Alliance to become the new Conservative Party.

Senate: the upper house of Parliament. Here, senators examine and revise legislation from the House of Commons, the lower house of Parliament, investigate national issues and represent regional, provincial and minority interests. Senate members can also introduce their own bills.

Social Credit Party: a former federal political party. It exists still as a provincial party in British Columbia. From 1935 to 1968, the federal Social Credit Party sent members to Parliament, mainly from Alberta, British Columbia, and Quebec. The party believed that the government should give people money so that they could afford to purchase the goods and services available in the community. This money was called "social credit".

Speech from the Throne: the speech made by the Queen's representative, the governor general (or lieutenant governor at the provincial level), at the opening of a parliamentary session. It explains the government's goals and how it plans to reach them. The speech is given in the Senate. There are a number of formalities that must be followed.

Thatcher, Margaret (1925–): prime minister of Great Britain (1979–1990). She was the first female to head a major Western democracy.

Tories: nickname of the Conservative party, in both Great Britain and Canada. It comes from the Irish word *tóraidhe*, which means pursuer or chaser. The term was originally used by the British to degrade the Roman Catholic Irish who robbed the English settlers and soldiers in Ireland. From 1689 it has been the name of the political party with conservative ideas and later as the party that is closely associated with the Church of England (Anglican).

Still more words and facts you might want to know

Trudeau, Pierre Elliott (1919–2000): 15th prime minister of Canada (1968–1979, 1980–1984). Pierre worked as a lawyer and law professor before he entered politics in 1965. He dealt with the kidnapping of a British diplomat and a Quebec Cabinet minister by invoking the War Measures Act in 1970. He worked to make the federal government bilingual and, in 1982, repatriated the Constitution from Great Britain so that Canada can make its own changes to it.

trustee: a school board trustee is an elected member of a group of citizens who work with school board employees to address issues about education in a local area. Trustees represent the people at board meetings and work to make changes that improve the educational experience for elementary and secondary students.

24 Sussex Drive: in Ottawa, the official residence of the prime minister of Canada since 1951. The house was built in 1866 by mill owner and member of Parliament Joseph Merrill Currier as a wedding gift to his bride Hannah. He called the home, "Gorffwysfa," a Welsh word meaning "place of peace."

USSR (Union of Soviet Socialist Republics): also known as the Soviet Union, the USSR was formed after the October Revolution in 1917. It was a popular region to travel to because it was the first government led by a Communist Party. In 1991, though, the USSR split into a number of separate countries, including Russia, Belarus, Ukraine, Moldova, Georgia, Armenia, Azerbaijan, and many others.

Vancouver Non-Partisan Association (NPA): an independent political organization made up of citizens who live, work, own businesses or properties in Vancouver. The mission of the group is to ensure that the government of Vancouver is responsible with its budgets.

Vander Zalm, Wilhelmus Nicholaas (Bill) (1934–): British Columbia's 28th premier (1986–1991). He resigned from politics in 1983, but came back into public life to succeed Bennett as leader of the Social Credit Party and premier in 1986. Scandal led to his resignation as premier in 1991.

Vietnam War (1954–1975): conflict that began with the military defeat of the French in their former colony of Vietnam. This was followed by communist North Vietnamese invading South Vietnam in hopes of reuniting the country. Fearing the spread of communism in the world, the U.S. sends troops to support the South Vietnamese army. American troops pulled out following the signing of the 1973 Paris Peace Accord. South Vietnam fell to the North when an armed revolt in the South was crushed following the North's refusal to hold free and democratic elections as had been promised.

West Indies: the string of islands in the Atlantic Ocean between Florida in North America and Venezuela in South America.

women's liberation movement: a movement in the late 1960s where women in developed countries fought for equal rights to men. Before the movement, women were paid less than men for the same work and had very little access to daycare services for their children. The women's liberation movement in the 1960s made it possible for women like Kim Campbell to become leaders in politics.

world's superpowers: a term used to describe powerful countries during the Cold War, namely the United States and the USSR.

Index